MW01628674

all shook up!

all shook up!

hamlyn

This edition first published in the U.K. in 1999 by
Hamlyn, a division of Octopus Publishing Group Limited
2–4 Heron Quays, London E14 4JP

Reprinted 2002

Printed in China

ISBN 0 600 60658 9

NOTES

Both metric and imperial measurements have been given in all recipes. Use one set of measurements only and not a mixture of both.

Standard level spoon measurements are used in all recipes.
1 tablespoon = one 15 ml spoon
1 teaspoon = one 5 ml spoon

Eggs should be medium to large unless otherwise stated. The Department of Health advises that eggs should not be consumed raw. This book contains dishes made with raw or lightly cooked eggs. It is prudent for more vulnerable people such as pregnant and nursing mothers, invalids, the elderly, babies and young children to avoid uncooked or lightly cooked dishes made with eggs. Once prepared, these dishes should be kept refrigerated and used promptly.

The measure that has been used in the cocktail recipes is based on a bar jigger, which is 45 ml/1½ fl oz. If preferred, a different volume can be used providing the proportions are kept constant within a drink and suitable adjustments are made to spoon measurements, where they occur.

Milk should be full fat unless otherwise stated.

Fresh fruit should be used, unless otherwise stated.

Measurements for canned food have been given as a standard metric equivalent.

Nuts and nut derivatives
This book includes dishes made with nuts and nut derivatives. It is advisable for customers with known allergic reactions to nuts and nut derivatives and those who may be potentially vulnerable to these allergies, such as pregnant and nursing mothers, invalids, the elderly, babies and children, to avoid dishes made with nuts and nut oils. It is also prudent to check the labels of pre-prepared ingredients for the possible inclusion of nut derivatives.

Contents

Introduction

There's virtually no social occasion which isn't enhanced by a drink, be it a powerful mint julep, a healthy smoothie or a steaming glass of hot spicy punch. Drinks, hot or cold, soothing or stimulating, and alcoholic or otherwise, oil the wheels of our social lives and add to its pleasure. The drinks in this collection range from a thirst-quenching Saffron Lassi from India to old-fashioned country favourites like home-made Lemonade and Lemon Barley Water, and from Coffee Diablo, a truly stimulating warmer in which black coffee is spiked with brandy, Cointreau, cloves and citrus rind, to potent cocktails such as the Alexander Baby whose deceptively mild appearance of cream sprinkled with nutmeg masks a heady combination of dark rum and chocolate flavoured liqueur. They are all equally delicious in their different ways and they all have their place in the social calendar.

COCKTAILS

The 1920s were the golden age of the cocktail. In England, in the early twenties, they were all the rage among the bright young things because they were new, extremely potent and originated in the USA, the home of all things sophisticated and enviable, and guaranteed to upset the older generation. However, the cocktail was quickly acclimatized and by the late twenties the cocktail party was an established part of the smart London social scene. It was the age that produced, among many others, the Bucks Fizz, Bloody Mary and Between the Sheets.

PUNCH

This dates back to an earlier era, to the days of the nabobs who made their fortunes in India in the eighteenth century. The name punch is said to come from *panch*, the Hindustani for five, referring to its five ingredients, arrack or spirit, lime or other citrus juice, sugar, spice and water. The definition of punch has broadened and punches can now be wine-based, cider-based or even non-alcoholic, and they may also be hot as well as cold. They are the simplest drink to serve at large parties as they can usually be prepared well in advance.

SMOOTHIES

These are the newest soft, cold drinks to reach us from the USA. Easily prepared from delicious combinations of fresh fruit and blended to a rich softness with ice cream, sorbets, yogurt, milk or coconut milk they are almost a meal in themselves and the answer to every busy parent's prayer since they are nutritious, satisfying and whizzed together in minutes.

BAR EQUIPMENT

To run a home bar efficiently, the major pieces of equipment required are a cocktail shaker, a mixing glass and a blender.

The **cocktail shaker**, which may be made of metal or acrylic and comes with its own built-in strainer, is for preparing drinks containing fruit juices, thick liqueurs and other ingredients which require a very thorough mixing. The ice which is added with the other ingredients serves partly to chill the drink and also adds as a beater in the shaker.

A **mixing glass**, sometimes called a **bar glass**, is used for drinks which are stirred rather than shaken. These are clear drinks whose appearance would be spoiled by vigorous shaking. They are then strained into fresh glasses. The mixing glass, which is used in conjunction with a long-handled bar spoon, is large enough to mix several drinks at the same time.

A **blender** or **food processor** is essential for making smoothies and other fruit-based drinks.

Bar measures, **ice containers**, **tongs** for lifting ice cubes and a **bar strainer** are also necessary. Other essential equipment will be found in every kitchen, i.e. chopping boards and sharp knives, a canelle knife for removing citrus rind, a lemon squeezer, ice trays, cocktail sticks, corkscrews, bottle openers and tea towels. Glass swizzle sticks, fancy drinking straws and little paper parasols all add to the fun of the occasion.

GLASSES

A well-mixed drink will taste good whatever it is presented in and a standard wine glass with a capacity of 150 ml/5 fl oz is perfectly suitable for almost any drink. However, some drinks are usually served in glasses of a particular shape.

The classic cocktail glass has a wide vee-shaped or shallow rounded bowl set on a long stem. The wide bowl provides scope for decorating the drink and the long stem enables the drinker to hold the glass without warming the drink. The Margarita glass also has a long stem but with a small bowl topped by a shallow saucer with a wide rim for the salt decoration. It has much the same capacity as a cocktail glass and the two are often used interchangeably. An old-fashioned glass is a short tumbler with a 175–200 ml/6–8 fl oz capacity and a highball glass is a straight-sided tumbler holding about 250 ml/8 fl oz. The hurricane glass, shaped like a hurricane lamp, is also for long drinks.

Hot drinks should be served in heatproof glasses, ideally with a handle, or in cups or mugs.

ICE

This is almost the most important ingredient in a cold drink or cocktail since virtually all cold drinks taste better when served ice cold. It really is

impossible to have too much ice on hand when mixing drinks but fortunately large supplies of ice can now be bought from wine merchants and off licences at a very reasonable price. By the same token, keep all your drinks in a cool, dark place and, if you can, store fruit juices and mixers in a refrigerator.

Recipes sometimes specify crushed ice or cracked ice. Crushed ice cools a drink more, and more quickly, than cracked ice but too much of it will dilute a drink too fast. Cracked ice is made by putting ice cubes into a strong polythene bag and hitting it with a rolling pin; for crushed ice, it is simply broken up more finely.

A glass should be cooled before serving an iced drink. To do this, put in some crushed ice and stir it around until the unside of the glass has cooled. Alternatively, place glasses in the refrigerator. For a frosty glass, put the glass in the freezer for a few minutes before pouring in the drink.

SUGAR SYRUP

This is used in many cocktails. It blends into a cold drink more quickly than sugar and gives it more body. It is very easy to make at home, simply put 4 tablespoons of caster sugar into a small saucepan with 4 tablespoons of water. Bring the mixture slowly to the boil, stirring all the time to dissolve the sugar, then boil without stirring for 1–2 minutes. Sugar syrup can be stored in a sterilized bottle in the refrigerator for up to 2 months.

DECORATIONS

Frivolous drinks lend themselves to frivolous decorations. Classic decorations for cocktails are thin slices of lemon, orange or lime, mint sprigs, cherries and green olives, singly or in combination, but slices of kiwi fruit, strawberries, hulled or unhulled, wedges or chunks of pineapple, cucumber and apple slices and tiny blue borage flowers also look enticing.

Citrus spirals are newer and more attractive than slices. Pare a long thin strand of rind from a lemon, lime or orange with a canelle knife or swivel-headed vegetable peeler, including a little pith with the zest to give it body, then wind the spiral round a glass swizzle stick or the handle of a wooden spoon. Drape the spiral over a glass or punch bowl, tie it in a decorative knot or loop it around a cherry.

Pieces of celery stick with lots of foliage traditionally accompany the Bloody Mary as a stirrer and cinnamon sticks serve the same purpose with hot punches. Creamy drinks can be sprinkled with nutmeg. Smoothies are topped with luscious ice cream and nuts.

The glass itself can also be decorated, rimmed with sugar, salt for a Margarita or with drinking chocolate powder as in the Crossbow on page 14. To do this, dampen the rim of the glass with water or citrus juice and invert the glass into a saucer of caster sugar, salt or drinking chocolate.

GLOSSARY

The following is a guide to some of the more unusual drinks used in this book.

Amaretto di Saronno
An Italian liqueur made from a combination of apricots and almonds.

Bitters
A powerful herbal or fruit-flavoured essence used in very small quantities to add distinctive flavour to drinks. Angostura bitters, the pink in pink gins, is herb flavoured although details of the recipe are a closely kept secret. Orange bitters are another favourite.

Cointreau
An orange flavoured liqueur.

Crème de cacao
A chocolate flavoured liqueur which comes in colourless and chocolate brown varieties.

Crème de cassis
A blackcurrant flavoured liqueur from France.

Curaçao
An orange flavoured liqueur from the Caribbean island that bears its name. It comes in several colours, including a vibrant blue, but the flavour is constant.

Kahlua
A coffee flavoured liqueur from Mexico.

Pernod
A French anis-flavoured spirit drunk as an aperitif. It is mixed with water which turns it a pale yellow colour and cloudy.

Sloe gin
A country liqueur made from gin flavoured with sugar and sloes.

Southern Comfort
A comparatively dry liqueur from the USA combining Bourbon whiskey with peaches, oranges and herbs.

Big Shots

Drink! for you know not whence
you came nor why:
Drink! for you know not why
you go, nor where.

Edward Fitzgerald
(1809–1883)

New Orleans Dry Martini *top left*

5–6 ice cubes
2–3 drops pernod
1 measure dry vermouth
4 measures gin

Put the ice cubes into a mixing glass. Pour the pernod over the ice, then pour in the vermouth and gin. Stir (never shake) vigorously and evenly without splashing. Strain into a chilled cocktail glass.

Preparation time: 3 minutes
Serves 1

Poet's Dream

4–5 ice cubes
1 measure Bénédictine
1 measure dry vermouth
3 measures gin
1 slice lemon rind

Put the ice cubes into a mixing glass. Pour the Bénédictine, vermouth and gin over the ice and stir vigorously, without splashing. Strain into a chilled cocktail glass. Twist the lemon rind over the drink, drop it in and serve.

Preparation time: 4 minutes
Serves 1

Zaza

5–6 ice cubes
3 drops orange bitters
1 measure Dubonnet
2 measures gin

Put the ice cubes into a mixing glass. Shake the bitters over the ice, pour in the Dubonnet and gin and stir vigorously without splashing. Strain into a chilled cocktail glass.

Preparation time: 3 minutes
Serves 1

Opera *bottom right*

4–5 ice cubes
1 measure Dubonnet
½ measure Curaçao
2 measures gin
orange rind spiral, to decorate

Put the ice cubes into a mixing glass. Pour the Dubonnet, Curaçao and gin over the ice. Stir evenly, then strain into a chilled cocktail glass. Decorate with the orange rind spiral and serve.

Preparation time: 3 minutes
Serves 1

Crossbow *top left*

4–5 ice cubes
½ measure gin
½ measure crème de cacao
½ measure Cointreau
drinking chocolate powder, to decorate

Put the ice cubes into a cocktail shaker and add the gin, crème de cacao and Cointreau. Dampen the rim of a chilled cocktail glass with a little water then dip the rim into a saucer of drinking chocolate. Shake the drink vigorously then strain into the glass.

Preparation time: 3 minutes
Serves 1

Kiss in the Dark

4–5 ice cubes
1 measure gin
1 measure cherry brandy
1 teaspoon dry vermouth

Put the ice cubes into a cocktail shaker and pour in the gin, cherry brandy and dry vermouth. Shake then strain into a chilled cocktail glass.

Preparation time: 2 minutes
Serves 1

Moon River

4–5 ice cubes
½ measure dry gin
½ measure apricot brandy
½ measure Cointreau
¼ measure Galliano
¼ measure fresh lemon juice
cocktail cherry, to decorate

Put some ice cubes into a mixing glass and pour in the gin, apricot brandy, Cointreau, Galliano and lemon juice. Stir then strain the drink into a large chilled cocktail glass. Decorate with the cherry and serve.

Preparation time: 3 minutes
Serves 4

Luigi *bottom right*

4–5 ice cubes
1 measure fresh orange juice
1 measure dry vermouth
½ measure Cointreau
1 measure grenadine
2 measures gin
orange slice, to decorate

Put the ice cubes into a mixing glass. Pour the orange juice, vermouth, Cointreau, grenadine and gin over the ice and stir vigorously. Strain into a chilled cocktail glass, decorate with the orange slice and serve.

Preparation time: 4 minutes
Serves 1

Manhattan *top left*

4–5 ice cubes
1 measure sweet vermouth
3 measures rye or bourbon whiskey
1 cocktail cherry, to decorate (optional)

Put the ice cubes into a mixing glass. Pour the vermouth and whiskey over the ice. Stir vigorously, then strain into a chilled cocktail glass. To serve, add a cherry if you like.

Preparation time: 3 minutes
Serves 1

Oriental

4–5 ice cubes
1 measure rye whiskey
½ measure sweet vermouth
½ measure Cointreau
½ measure fresh lime juice

Put the ice cubes into a cocktail shaker and pour the whiskey, vermouth, Cointreau and lime juice over the ice. Shake then strain into a chilled cocktail glass.

Preparation time: 4 minutes
Serves 1

Whizz Bang

4–5 ice cubes
3 drops orange bitters
½ teaspoon grenadine
1 measure dry vermouth
3 measures Scotch whisky
1 drop pernod

Put the ice cubes into a mixing glass. Shake the orange bitters over the ice and pour in the grenadine, vermouth and whisky. Stir vigorously then strain into a chilled cocktail glass. Add the pernod and serve.

Preparation time: 4 minutes
Serves 1

Cassis Cocktail *bottom right*

4–5 ice cubes
1 measure bourbon whiskey
½ measure dry vermouth
1 teaspoon crème de cassis
2 blueberries, to decorate

Put the ice cubes into a cocktail shaker and pour in the bourbon, vermouth and crème de cassis. Shake the drink then strain into a chilled cocktail glass and decorate with the blueberries impaled on a cocktail stick.

Preparation time: 3 minutes
Serves 1

Morning *top left*

4–5 ice cubes
3 drops Angostura bitters
5 drops pernod
½ teaspoon grenadine
½ teaspoon dry vermouth
1 measure Curaçao
3 measures brandy
cocktail cherries, to serve

Put the ice cubes into a mixing glass. Shake the bitters over the ice, and add the pernod. Pour in the grenadine, vermouth, Curaçao and brandy, stir vigorously then strain into a chilled cocktail glass and decorate with cocktail cherries.

Preparation time: 3 minutes
Serves 1

Toulon

4–5 ice cubes
1 measure dry vermouth
1 measure Bénédictine
3 measures brandy
1 piece of orange rind, to decorate

Put the ice cubes into a mixing glass. Pour the vermouth, Bénédictine and brandy over the ice and stir vigorously. Strain into a chilled cocktail glass and decorate with the orange rind.

Preparation time: 3 minutes
Serves 1

Melbourne

4–5 ice cubes
1 measure Curaçao
3 measures brandy
1 piece of lemon rind

Put the ice cubes into a measuring glass, pour over the Curaçao and brandy and stir vigorously. Strain into a chilled cocktail glass. Twist the lemon rind over the drink then drop it in.

Preparation time: 3 minutes
Serves 1

Burnt Orange *bottom right*

4–5 ice cubes
3 drops orange bitters or Angostura bitters
juice of ½ orange
3 measures brandy
orange slice, to decorate

Put the ice cubes into a mixing glass. Shake the bitters over the ice, add the orange juice and brandy and stir vigorously. Strain into a chilled cocktail glass and serve decorated with an orange slice.

Preparation time: 2 minutes
Serves 1

American Beauty *top left*

4–5 ice cubes
1 measure brandy
1 measure dry vermouth
1 measure fresh orange juice
1 measure grenadine
1 dash crème de menthe
ruby port

TO DECORATE:
cocktail cherry
orange slice
mint sprig

Put the ice cubes into a cocktail shaker and pour in the brandy, vermouth, orange juice, grenadine and crème de menthe. Shake well and strain into a cocktail glass. Tilt the glass and gently pour in a little ruby port so that it floats on top. Decorate with a cocktail cherry, orange slice and mint sprig on a cocktail stick.

Preparation time: 4 minutes
Serves 1

Alexander's Sister

4–5 ice cubes
1 measure brandy
1 measure Kahlúa
1 measure double cream
grated nutmeg

Put the ice cubes into a cocktail shaker. Pour the brandy, Kahlúa and cream over the ice cubes and shake well. Strain into a cocktail glass and sprinkle with grated nutmeg.

Preparation time: 3 minutes
Serves 1

Depth Bomb

4–5 ice cubes
juice of 1 lemon
½ teaspoon grenadine
1 measure Calvados
2 measures brandy
slices of red- or green-skinned apple, to decorate

Put the ice cubes into a mixing glass. Pour the lemon juice, grenadine, Calvados and brandy over the ice and stir vigorously. Strain into a chilled cocktail glass and decorate with slices of apple.

Preparation time: 3 minutes
Serves 1

Banana Bliss *bottom right*

4–5 ice cubes
1 measure brandy
1 measure crème de banane
1 measure Cointreau
banana slice
lemon juice

Put the ice cubes into a mixing glass and pour in the brandy, crème de banane and Cointreau. Stir with a spoon then strain into a cocktail glass. Dip the banana into lemon juice to prevent it discolouring then attach it to the rim of the glass.

Preparation time: 4 minutes
Serves 1

Port Antonio *left*

½ teaspoon grenadine
4–5 ice cubes
1 measure fresh lime juice
3 measures white or golden rum

TO DECORATE:
lime rind
cocktail cherry

Spoon the grenadine into a chilled cocktail glass. Put the ice cubes into a mixing glass. Pour the lime juice and rum over the ice and stir vigorously then strain into the cocktail glass. Wrap the lime rind round the cocktail cherry, impale them with a cocktail stick and use to decorate the drink.

Preparation time: 3 minutes
Serves 1

Rum Sidecar

4–5 ice cubes
juice of 1 lemon
1 measure Cointreau
3 measures white or golden rum

Put the ice cubes into a mixing glass and pour in the lemon juice, Cointreau and rum. Stir vigorously then strain into a chilled cocktail glass.

Preparation time: 4 minutes
Serves 1

Rum Martini

4–5 ice cubes
1 measure dry vermouth
3 measures white rum
1 piece of lemon rind

Put the ice cubes into a mixing glass. Pour the vermouth and rum over the ice, stir vigorously then strain into a chilled cocktail glass. Twist the lemon rind over the drink and drop it in.

Preparation time: 2 minutes
Serves 1

Grenada Cocktail *right*

4–5 ice cubes
juice of ½ orange
1 measure sweet vermouth
3 measures golden or dark rum
small pieces of cinnamon stick, to decorate (optional)

Put the ice cubes into a mixing glass. Pour the orange juice, vermouth and rum over the ice, stir vigorously then strain into a cocktail glass and decorate with small pieces of cinnamon stick.

Preparation time: 2 minutes
Serves 1

Black Widow *top left*

4–5 ice cubes
2 measures dark rum
1 measure Southern Comfort
juice of ½ lime
1 dash sugar syrup
lime slice, to decorate

Put the ice cubes into a cocktail shaker. Pour in the rum, Southern Comfort, lime juice and sugar syrup and shake well. Strain into a chilled cocktail glass and decorate with a lime slice.

Preparation time: 2 minutes
Serves 1

Honeysuckle

4–5 ice cubes
2 measures golden rum
juice of 1 lime
1 teaspoon clear honey

Put the ice cubes into a cocktail shaker. Pour in the rum and lime juice and add the honey. Shake well then strain into a cocktail glass.

Preparation time: 3 minutes
Serves 1

Bahamas

4–5 ice cubes
1 measure white rum
1 measure Southern Comfort
1 measure fresh lemon juice
1 dash crème de banane
thin lemon slice, to decorate

Put some ice cubes into a cocktail shaker and pour in the rum, Southern Comfort, lemon juice and crème de banane. Shake vigorously then strain into a chilled cocktail glass. Drop in a thin lemon slice and serve.

Preparation time: 3 minutes
Serves 1

Alexander Baby *bottom right*

4–5 ice cubes
2 measures dark rum
1 measure crème de cacao
½ measure double cream
grated nutmeg

Put the ice cubes into a cocktail shaker and pour the rum, crème de cacao and cream over the ice. Shake the drink then strain it into a chilled cocktail glass. Sprinkle grated nutmeg on top.

Preparation time: 3 minutes
Serves 1

Xantippe *top left*

4–5 ice cubes
1 measure cherry brandy
1 measure yellow Chartreuse
2 measures vodka

Put the ice cubes into a mixing glass. Pour the cherry brandy, Chartreuse and vodka over the ice and stir vigorously. Strain into a chilled cocktail glass.

Preparation time: 2 minutes
Serves 1

Inspiration

4–5 ice cubes
½ measure Bénédictine
½ measure dry vermouth
2 measures vodka
1 lime rind spiral, to decorate

Put the ice cubes into a mixing glass. Pour the Bénédictine, vermouth and vodka over the ice. Stir vigorously then strain into a chilled cocktail glass and decorate with the lime spiral.

Preparation time: 3 minutes
Serves 1

Cool Wind

4–5 ice cubes
1 measure dry vermouth
juice of ½ grapefruit
½ teaspoon Cointreau
3 measures vodka

Put the ice cubes into a mixing glass. Pour the vermouth, grapefruit juice, Cointreau and vodka over the ice. Stir gently then strain into a chilled cocktail glass.

Preparation time: 3 minutes
Serves 1

Haven *bottom right*

2–3 ice cubes
1 tablespoon grenadine
1 measure pernod
1 measure vodka
soda water

Put the ice cubes into an old-fashioned glass. Dash the grenadine over the ice, then pour in the pernod and vodka. Top up with soda water and serve.

Preparation time: 3 minutes
Serves 1

Pancho Villa *top left*

4–5 ice cubes
1 measure tequila
½ measure Tia Maria
1 teaspoon Cointreau

Put the ice cubes into a cocktail shaker and pour in the tequila, Tia Maria and Cointreau. Shake the drink then strain it into a chilled cocktail glass.

Preparation time: 3 minutes
Serves 1

Frostbite

4–5 ice cubes
1 measure tequila
1 measure double cream
1 measure white crème de cacao
grated nutmeg

Put the ice cubes into a cocktail shaker. Pour the tequila, cream and crème de cacao over the ice. Shake the drink then strain it into a cocktail glass. Sprinkle with grated nutmeg.

Preparation time: 3 minutes
Serves 1

Frozen Strawberry

a small handful of crushed ice
1 measure tequila
1 measure strawberry liqueur
1 dash fresh lemon juice
4 ripe strawberries
fresh strawberry, to decorate

Put the crushed ice into a blender and pour in the tequila, strawberry liqueur and lemon juice. Drop in the strawberries and blend for a few seconds. Pour without straining into a cocktail glass and decorate with a strawberry.

Preparation time: 3 minutes
Serves 1

Margarita *bottom right*

There are many versions of the Margarita but this is one of the most popular. Reduce the amount of lemon juice, if you prefer.

4–5 ice cubes
1 measure tequila
1 measure fresh lemon or lime juice, plus extra for glass rim
½ measure Cointreau

TO DECORATE:
salt for glass rim
lemon or lime slice

Dampen the rim of a cocktail or margarita glass with lemon or lime juice and dip it into fine salt to frost. Put the ice cubes into a cocktail shaker. Pour in the tequila, lemon or lime juice and Cointreau and shake. Strain into the glass and decorate with a lemon or lime slice.

Preparation time: 4 minutes
Serves 1

Long Shots

There's many a slip 'twixt
the cup and the lip.

Proverb

Sea Breeze *top left*

6–8 ice cubes
½ measure fresh grapefruit juice
½ measure cranberry juice
1 measure dry vermouth
3 measures gin
lime slice, to decorate

Put 2–3 ice cubes into a mixing glass. Pour the grapefruit juice, cranberry juice, vermouth and gin over the ice then stir gently. Put 4–5 fresh ice cubes into a chilled hurricane glass and strain the drink over the ice. Decorate with a lime slice.

Preparation time: 5 minutes
Serves 1

Gin Floradora

4–5 ice cubes
½ teaspoon sugar syrup
juice of ½ lime
½ teaspoon grenadine
2 measures gin
dry ginger ale
twist of lime rind, to decorate

Put the ice cubes into a cocktail shaker. Pour in the sugar syrup, lime juice, grenadine and gin and shake until a froth forms. Pour without straining into a hurricane glass. Top up with dry ginger ale, decorate with a lime twist and serve.

Preparation time: 3 minutes
Serves 1

John Collins

5–6 ice cubes
1 teaspoon sugar syrup
1 measure lemon juice
3 measures gin
soda water

TO DECORATE:
1 lemon slice
1 mint sprig

Put the ice cubes into a cocktail shaker. Pour in the sugar syrup, lemon juice and gin and shake vigorously until a frost forms. Pour without straining into a Collins glass. Add the lemon and mint and top up with soda water. Stir gently and serve.

Preparation time: 5 minutes
Serves 1

Singapore Gin Sling

bottom right

6–8 ice cubes
juice of ½ lemon
juice of ½ orange
1 measure cherry brandy
3 measures gin
3 drops Angostura bitters
soda water
1 lemon slice, to decorate

Put 4–6 ice cubes into a cocktail shaker. Pour the lemon and orange juices, cherry brandy and gin over the ice and add the bitters. Shake the mixture until a frost forms. Put 2 fresh ice cubes into a hurricane glass. Pour the cocktail without straining into the glass and top up with soda water. Decorate with the lemon slice and serve.

Preparation time: 5 minutes
Serves 1

Gin Tropical *top left*

8–10 ice cubes
1½ measures gin
1 measure fresh lemon juice
1 measure passion fruit juice
½ measure orange juice
soda water
orange rind spiral, to decorate

Put 4–5 ice cubes into a cocktail shaker, pour in the gin, lemon juice, passion fruit juice and orange juice and shake well. Put 4–5 fresh ice cubes into an old-fashioned glass and strain the cocktail over the ice. Top up with soda water and stir gently. Decorate with an orange rind spiral.

Preparation time: 5 minutes
Serves 1

Albemarle Fizz

8–10 ice cubes
1 measure gin
juice of ½ lemon
2 dashes raspberry syrup
½ teaspoon sugar syrup
soda water
cocktail cherries, to decorate

Put 4–5 ice cubes into a mixing glass and add the gin, lemon juice, raspberry syrup and sugar syrup. Stir to mix then strain into a highball glass. Add 4–5 fresh ice cubes and top up with soda water. Decorate with two cherries impaled on a cocktail stick and serve with straws.

Preparation time: 5 minutes
Serves 1

Sydney Fizz

4–5 ice cubes
1 measure fresh lemon juice
1 measure fresh orange juice
½ teaspoon grenadine
3 measures gin
soda water
orange slice, to decorate

Put the ice cubes into a cocktail shaker. Pour the lemon and orange juices, grenadine and gin over the ice and shake vigorously until a frost forms. Strain into an old-fashioned glass. Top up with soda water, add the orange slice and serve.

Preparation time: 4 minutes
Serves 1

Cherry Julep *bottom right*

3–4 ice cubes
juice of ½ lemon
1 teaspoon sugar syrup
1 teaspoon grenadine
1 measure cherry brandy
1 measure sloe gin
2 measures gin
chopped ice
lemon rind strips, to decorate

Put the ice cubes into a cocktail shaker. Pour the lemon juice, sugar syrup, grenadine, cherry brandy, sloe gin and gin over the ice. Fill a highball glass with finely chopped ice. Shake the mixture until a frost forms then strain it and pour into the ice-filled glass. Decorate with lemon rind strips and serve.

Preparation time: 5 minutes
Serves 1

Juliana Blue *top left*

crushed ice
1 measure gin
½ measure Cointreau
½ measure blue Curaçao
2 measures pineapple juice
½ measure fresh lime juice
1 measure cream of coconut
1–2 ice cubes

TO DECORATE:
pineapple slice
cocktail cherries

Put some crushed ice into a blender and pour in the gin, Cointreau, blue Curaçao, pineapple and lime juices and cream of coconut. Blend at high speed for several seconds until the mixture has a consistency of soft snow. Put the ice cubes into a cocktail glass and strain the mixture on to them. Decorate with a pineapple slice and cocktail cherries. Serve with straws.

Preparation time: 5 minutes
Serves 1

Gin Cooler

3–4 ice cubes
½ teaspoon grenadine
juice of 1 lemon
3 measures gin
soda water

TO DECORATE:
1 cocktail cherry
1 lemon slice

Put the ice cubes into a highball glass. Pour the grenadine over the ice, then the lemon juice and the gin and stir evenly allowing the mixture to blend. Top up the drink with soda water. Decorate with a cocktail cherry and a lemon slice.

Preparation time: 5 minutes
Serves 1

Golden Dawn

4–5 ice cubes
juice of ½ orange
1 measure Calvados
1 measure apricot brandy
3 measures gin
soda water
skewered orange rind, to decorate

Put the ice cubes into a cocktail shaker. Pour the orange juice, Calvados, apricot brandy and gin over the ice and shake until a frost forms. Strain into a highball glass, top up with soda water and decorate with orange rind.

Preparation time: 4 minutes
Serves 1

Honolulu *bottom right*

4–5 ice cubes
1 measure pineapple juice
1 measure fresh lemon juice
1 measure fresh orange juice
½ teaspoon grenadine
3 measures gin

TO DECORATE:
pineapple slice
cocktail cherry

Put the ice cubes into a cocktail shaker. Pour the pineapple, lemon and orange juices, the grenadine and gin over the ice and shake until a frost forms. Strain the drink into a chilled cocktail glass and decorate with the pineapple and cherry.

Preparation time: 4 minutes
Serves 1

Benedict *left*

3–4 ice cubes
1 measure Bénédictine
3 measures Scotch whisky
dry ginger ale

Put the ice cubes into a mixing glass. Pour the Bénédictine and whisky over the ice. Stir evenly without splashing and, without straining, pour the cocktail into a chilled highball glass. Top up with dry ginger ale and serve.

Preparation time: 3 minutes
Serves 1

Mississippi Punch

crushed ice
3 drops Angostura bitters
1 teaspoon sugar syrup
juice of 1 lemon
1 measure brandy
1 measure dark rum
2 measures bourbon or Scotch whisky

Fill a highball glass with crushed ice. Shake the bitters over the ice and pour in the sugar syrup and lemon juice. Stir gently to mix thoroughly. Add the brandy, rum and whisky, in that order, stir once and serve with drinking straws.

Preparation time: 4 minutes
Serves 1

Nerida

4–5 ice cubes
juice of ½ lime or lemon
3 measures Scotch whisky
dry ginger ale
lime or lemon slices, to decorate

Put the ice cubes into a cocktail shaker. Pour the lime or lemon juice and whisky over the ice. Shake until a frost forms then pour without straining into a chilled Collins glass. Top up with ginger ale and stir gently. Decorate with lime or lemon slices and serve.

Preparation time: 4 minutes
Serves 1

Louisville Mint Julep

right

1 teaspoon sugar syrup
3 young mint sprigs, extra to decorate
crushed ice
3 measures bourbon or Scotch whisky

Put the sugar syrup into an old-fashioned glass. Add the mint and stir to mix it gently with the sugar. Pack crushed ice into the glass. Pour the whisky over the ice, stirring it gently. Add more crushed ice and stir until a frost forms, then top with the extra mint sprigs. Wrap the glass with a table napkin but do not touch the glass with your bare fingers or the frost will disappear.

Preparation time: 5 minutes
Serves 1

Acapulco *top left*

crushed ice
1 measure tequila
1 measure white rum
2 measures pineapple juice
1 measure fresh grapefruit juice
1 measure coconut milk
pineapple wedge, to decorate

Put some crushed ice into a cocktail shaker and pour in the tequila, rum, pineapple juice, grapefruit juice and coconut milk. Shake the drink then pour it into a hurricane glass and decorate with a pineapple wedge. Serve with straws.

Preparation time: 4 minutes
Serves 1

Azteca

handful of crushed ice
1 measure tequila
juice of ½ lime
½ teaspoon sugar syrup
1 small mango, peeled and stoned
4–5 ice cubes
½ lime slice, to decorate

Put a handful of crushed ice into a blender. Add the tequila, lime juice, sugar syrup and mango and blend for a few seconds. Put 4–5 ice cubes into a large cocktail glass then strain the drink over the ice. Decorate with the lime slice and serve with short straws.

Preparation time: 5 minutes
Serves 1

Coconut Tequila

a small handful of crushed ice
1 measure tequila
½ measure fresh lemon juice
½ measure coconut milk
3 dashes maraschino
lemon slice, to decorate

Put the crushed ice into a blender and add the tequila, lemon juice, coconut milk and maraschino. Blend for a few seconds then pour into a highball glass and decorate with a lemon slice.

Preparation time: 3 minutes
Serves 1

Tequila Sunset *bottom right*

1 measure gold tequila
5 measures fresh lemon juice
1 measure fresh orange juice
2 tablespoons honey
crushed ice
lemon rind spiral, to decorate

Put the tequila into a chilled cocktail glass, add the lemon juice and then orange juice and stir. Drizzle the honey into glass so that it falls in a layer to the bottom, add the crushed ice and decorate with a lemon rind spiral.

Preparation time: 4 minutes
Serves 1

St Lucia *top left*

4–5 ice cubes
1 measure Curaçao
1 measure dry vermouth
juice of ½ orange
1 teaspoon grenadine
2 measures white or golden rum

TO DECORATE:
orange rind spiral
cocktail cherry

Put the ice cubes into a cocktail shaker. Pour the Curaçao, vermouth, orange juice, grenadine and rum over the ice. Shake until a frost forms then pour without straining into a highball glass. To serve, decorate with an orange rind spiral and a cocktail cherry.

Preparation time: 3 minutes
Serves 1

Havana Zombie

4–5 ice cubes
juice of 1 lime
5 tablespoons pineapple juice
1 teaspoon sugar syrup
1 measure white rum
1 measure golden rum
1 measure dark rum

Put the ice cubes into a mixing glass. Pour the lime juice and pineapple juice, sugar syrup and rums over the ice and stir vigorously. Pour without straining into a tall glass.

Preparation time: 4 minutes
Serves 1

St James

3–4 ice cubes
juice of ½ lime or lemon
juice of 1 orange
3 drops Angostura bitters
2 measures white or golden rum
2 measures tonic water
1 lime or lemon slice

Put the ice cubes into a highball glass and pour in the lime or lemon juice and the orange juice. Shake the bitters on the ice, add the rum and tonic water and decorate with a lime or lemon slice. Stir gently and serve.

Preparation time: 3 minutes
Serves 1

Astronaut *bottom right*

8–10 ice cubes
½ measure white rum
½ measure vodka
½ measure fresh lemon juice
1 dash passion fruit juice
lemon wedge, to decorate

Put 4–5 ice cubes into a cocktail shaker and add the rum, vodka, lemon and passion fruit juices. Fill an old-fashioned glass with 4–5 fresh ice cubes. Shake the drink then strain it into the glass. Decorate with the lemon wedge and serve.

Preparation time: 4 minutes
Serves 1

BONZER
MADE IN
25ml

Pussyfoot *top left*

Although there is a well-known non-alcoholic Pussyfoot cocktail, this is a more potent version with a generous measure of white rum.

crushed ice
1½ measures white rum
1 measure double cream
1 measure pineapple juice
1 measure fresh lime juice
1 measure cherry juice

TO DECORATE:
pineapple slice
cocktail cherry

Put some crushed ice into a blender and add the rum, cream, pineapple juice, lime juice and cherry juice. Blend for 15–20 seconds then pour into a hurricane glass. Decorate with a pineapple slice and a cherry.

Preparation time: 3 minutes
Serves 1

Acapulco Gold

8–10 ice cubes
½ measure golden rum
½ measure tequila
1 measure pineapple juice
½ measure fresh grapefruit juice
½ measure cream of coconut

Put 4–5 ice cubes into a cocktail shaker. Pour in the rum, tequila, pineapple and grapefruit juices and cream of coconut. Put 4–5 fresh ice cubes into an old-fashioned glass and strain the cocktail over the ice.

Preparation time: 4 minutes
Serves 1

Banana Royal

crushed ice
1½ measures coconut milk
3 measures pineapple juice
1½ measures golden rum
½ measure double cream
1 ripe banana
grated coconut, to decorate

Put some crushed ice into a blender and add the coconut milk, pineapple juice, rum, cream and banana. Blend for 15–30 seconds until smooth and creamy. Pour into an old-fashioned glass and sprinkle with grated coconut.

Preparation time: 4 minutes
Serves 1

White Witch *bottom right*

8–10 ice cubes
1 measure white rum
½ measure white crème de cacao
½ measure Cointreau
juice of ½ lime
soda water

TO DECORATE:
orange slice
lime slice

Put 4–5 ice cubes into a cocktail shaker and pour in the rum, crème de cacao, Cointreau and lime juice. Put 4–5 fresh ice cubes into an old-fashioned glass. Shake the drink then strain it into the glass. Top up with soda water and stir to mix. Decorate with slices of orange and lime and serve with straws.

Preparation time: 4 minutes
Serves 1

Blue Hawaiian *top left*

crushed ice
1 measure white rum
½ measure blue Curaçao
2 measures pineapple juice
1 measure cream of coconut
pineapple wedge, to decorate

Put some crushed ice into a blender and pour in the rum, blue Curaçao, pineapple juice and cream of coconut. Blend for 20–30 seconds. Pour into a chilled cocktail glass and decorate with a piece of pineapple.

Preparation time: 3 minutes
Serves 1

Apricot Daiquiri

crushed ice
1 measure white rum
1 measure lemon juice
½ measure apricot liqueur or brandy
3 ripe apricots, skinned and stoned

TO DECORATE:
slice of apricot
cocktail cherry
mint sprig

Put some crushed ice into a blender. Add the rum, lemon juice, apricot liqueur or brandy and the apricots and blend for 1 minute or until the mixture is smooth. Pour into a chilled cocktail glass and decorate with an apricot slice, cherry and mint sprig.

Preparation time: 5 minutes
Serves 1

Coco Loco

Coconut water is the thin liquid found sloshing around inside a fresh coconut, whereas coconut milk is made by blending fresh coconut, grated coconut cream or desiccated coconut with hot water. Both coconut water and coconut milk are sold in cans.

crushed ice
4 measures coconut water
1 measure coconut milk
1 measure apricot brandy
1 measure white rum
ground cinnamon

Put some crushed ice into a blender and add the coconut water, coconut milk, apricot brandy and rum and blend at high speed. To serve, pour into a coconut shell and sprinkle with cinnamon.

Preparation time: 5 minutes
Serves 1

Frozen Pineapple Daiquiri *bottom right*

crushed ice
2–3 pineapple slices
½ measure fresh lime juice
1 measure white rum
¼ measure Cointreau
1 teaspoon sugar syrup
piece of pineapple, to decorate

Put some crushed ice into a blender and add the pineapple slices, lime juice, white rum, Cointreau and sugar syrup. Blend at the highest speed until smooth then pour into a chilled cocktail glass. Decorate with a piece of pineapple and serve with a straw.

Preparation time: 4 minutes
Serves 1

Between the Sheets *left*

4–5 ice cubes
1¼ measures brandy
1 measure white rum
½ measure Cointreau
¾ measure fresh lemon juice
½ measure sugar syrup

Put the ice cubes into a cocktail shaker. Add the brandy, white rum, Cointreau, lemon juice and sugar syrup and shake until a frost forms. Strain into a chilled cocktail glass.

Preparation time: 4 minutes
Serves 1

Penguin

1 measure brandy
½ measure Cointreau
1 measure fresh lemon juice
1 measure fresh orange juice
1 dash grenadine
ice cubes

TO DECORATE:
¼ orange slice
¼ lemon slice

Pour the brandy, Cointreau, lemon juice, orange juice and grenadine into a mixing glass and stir well. Fill a tall glass with ice cubes. Pour the drink into the glass and decorate with the quartered slices of orange and lemon placed on the rim of the glass. Serve with 2 long straws.

Preparation time: 4 minutes
Serves 1

Tinker

4–5 ice cubes
juice of ½ lime or lemon
3 measures brandy
dry ginger ale
skewered cucumber skin, to decorate

Put the ice cubes into a cocktail shaker, add the lime or lemon juice and brandy and shake until a frost forms. Pour, without straining, into a highball glass. Top up with dry ginger ale and serve decorated with skewered cucumber skin.

Preparation time: 4 minutes
Serves 1

American Rose *right*

4–5 ice cubes
1 measure brandy
1 dash pernod
1 dash grenadine
½ ripe peach, skinned, stoned and roughly chopped
crushed ice
Champagne
peach or mango slices, to decorate

Put the ice cubes into a cocktail shaker. Pour in the brandy, pernod and grenadine and add the peach. Fill a cocktail glass with crushed ice. Shake the mixture well then strain into the glass. Top up with Champagne just before serving and add the peach or mango slices.

Preparation time: 5 minutes
Serves 1

Bloody Mary *top left*

4–5 ice cubes
juice of ½ lemon
½ teaspoon horseradish sauce
2 drops Worcestershire sauce
1 drop Tabasco sauce
2 measures thick tomato juice
2 measures vodka
pinches of salt and pepper

TO DECORATE:
celery stick, with the leaves left on
lemon slice (optional)

Put the ice cubes into a cocktail shaker. Pour the lemon juice, horseradish sauce, Worcestershire sauce, Tabasco sauce, tomato juice and vodka over the ice. Shake until a frost forms. Pour into a tall glass, add a pinch of salt and pepper and decorate with a celery stick and a lemon slice, if you like.

Preparation time: 3 minutes
Serves 1

Frozen Steppes

1 measure vodka
1 measure dark crème de cacao
1 scoop vanilla ice cream
cocktail cherry, to decorate

Pour the vodka, crème de cacao and ice cream into a blender and blend for a few seconds. Pour the drink into a large wine glass and decorate with a cherry.

Preparation time: 3 minutes
Serves 1

Head-over-Heels

4–5 ice cubes
juice of 1 lime or lemon
1 teaspoon sugar syrup
3 measures vodka
3 drops Angostura bitters
Champagne
whole strawberry, to decorate

Put the ice cubes into a cocktail shaker. Pour the lime or lemon juice, sugar syrup, vodka and bitters over the ice and shake until a frost begins to form. Pour without straining into a highball glass, top up with Champagne and decorate with a strawberry.

Preparation time: 5 minutes
Serves 1

Vodka Sour *bottom right*

4–5 ice cubes
2 measures vodka
½ measure sugar syrup
1 egg white
1½ measures fresh lemon juice
3 drops Angostura bitters, to decorate

Put the ice cubes into a cocktail shaker, add the vodka, sugar syrup, egg white and lemon juice and shake until a frost forms. Pour without straining into a cocktail glass and shake 3 drops of Angostura bitters on the top to decorate.

Preparation time: 4 minutes
Serves 1

Warmers and Refreshers

Coffee, which makes
the politician wise,
And see through all things
with half-shut eyes.

Alexander Pope

(1688–1744)

Island Cream Grog *top left*

2 measures rum
200 ml/7 fl oz boiling water
sugar, to taste
whipped cream
grated nutmeg

Warm a heatproof handled glass and pour in the rum and boiling water. Add sugar to taste and stir. Spoon some whipped cream on top and sprinkle with grated nutmeg.

Preparation time: 4 minutes
Serves 1

Scotch Milk

2 measures Scotch whisky
1 measure Drambuie
5 measures hot milk
1 teaspoon finely granulated white sugar
1 pinch ground cinnamon

Pour the Scotch, Drambuie and hot milk into a mug. Add the sugar and cinnamon and stir together.

Preparation time: 3 minutes
Serves 1

Hot Brandy Punch

rind and juice of 2 lemons
10 cm/4 inch cinnamon stick
generous grating of nutmeg
6 cloves
6 tablespoons sugar syrup
300 ml/½ pint boiling water
1 bottle brandy

Put the lemon rind, cinnamon, nutmeg, cloves, sugar syrup and boiling water into a saucepan and simmer for 10 minutes. Strain into a warmed heatproof punch bowl and add the lemon juice and brandy. Set the punch alight and ladle into warmed mugs.

Preparation time: 5 minutes
Cooking time: 10 minutes
Serves 8–10

Sunset Tea *bottom right*

200 ml/7 fl oz freshly brewed Indian tea
½ measure golden rum
1 measure Cointreau
2 measures fresh orange juice

TO DECORATE:
orange slices stuck with 3 cloves
cinnamon sticks

Pour the tea into 2 heatproof glasses. Put the rum, Cointreau and orange juice into a small saucepan. Place it over a low heat and bring the mixture to just under boiling point, stirring constantly. Pour immediately into the glasses with the tea. Decorate with a slice of orange stuck with 3 cloves, and a cinnamon stick.

Preparation time: 5 minutes
Cooking time: 5 minutes
Serves 2

Coffee Amaretto *top left*

hot black coffee
½ measure Amaretto di Saronno
½ measure Tia Maria or Kahlúa
whipped cream
amaretti biscuits, to serve

Put some very hot black coffee into a mug or a heatproof handled glass and add the Amaretto and Tia Maria or Kahlúa. Stir well then spoon some whipped cream on top. Serve with amaretti biscuits.

Preparation time: 5 minutes
Serves 1

Irish Coffee

hot strong black coffee
1 teaspoon sugar (or more to taste)
1 measure Irish whiskey
double cream

Warm a heatproof handled glass then fill it three-quarters full of hot strong coffee. Add the sugar and whiskey and stir to mix. Carefully pour in some double cream over the back of a spoon so that it floats on top.

Preparation time: 5 minutes
Serves 1

Chocolate Punch

300 ml/½ pint milk
3 teaspoons cocoa powder
1 teaspoon instant coffee powder
1 teaspoon sugar
1 measure Kahlúa
whipped cream
ground cinnamon

Heat all the ingredients except the whipped cream and cinnamon in a small pan. Whisk together until well mixed. Just before the mixture comes to the boil pour into 2 heatproof glasses with handles. Spoon some whipped cream on top and sprinkle with ground cinnamon.

Preparation time: 5 minutes
Cooking time: 5 minutes
Serves 2

Coffee Diablo *bottom right*

hot black coffee
1 measure brandy
½ measure Cointreau
2 cloves
1 piece of orange rind
1 piece of lemon rind

Make enough hot black coffee to fill a heatproof handled glass three-quarters full. Pour the brandy and Cointreau into a small saucepan and add the cloves and orange and lemon rind. Put the pan over a low heat. Just before the mixture comes to the boil set it alight with a long taper and pour it flaming over the coffee. Serve at once.

Preparation time: 5 minutes
Cooking time: 5 minutes
Serves 1

Vanilla Coffee *left*

300 ml/½ pint milk
1 vanilla pod
600 ml/1 pint strong, hot black coffee
grated nutmeg

Put the milk into a saucepan and add the vanilla pod. Heat the milk until hot, but do not boil. Remove from the heat and leave to infuse for 5 minutes. Remove and discard the vanilla pod. Pour the hot coffee into four warmed heatproof glasses, cups or mugs and pour over the vanilla-flavoured milk. Sprinkle with grated nutmeg and serve.

Preparation time: 5 minutes, plus infusing
Cooking time: 5 minutes
Serves 4

Café Liégeois

300 ml/½ pint chilled black coffee
crushed ice
2 scoops coffee ice cream
whipped cream, to serve
1 teaspoon grated nutmeg
crumbled chocolate flake, to serve

Put the coffee, ice and ice cream into a food processor or blender and process briefly until thick and creamy. Pour into 2 tall glasses and top with whipped cream and grated nutmeg. Decorate with the crumbled chocolate flake.

Preparation time: 5 minutes
Serves 2

Orange Coffee

600 ml/1 pint strong black coffee
rind of ½ orange, in 1 piece
10 cm/4 inch cinnamon stick, broken in half
1 teaspoon grated nutmeg
clear honey or sugar, to taste
ice cubes or crushed ice, to serve

Put the coffee into a saucepan with the orange rind, cinnamon, nutmeg and honey or sugar to taste and simmer gently for 5–10 minutes. Remove the coffee from the heat and leave to cool. To serve, discard the cinnamon and orange peel and serve chilled over ice.

Preparation time: 5 minutes
Cooking time: 5–10 minutes
Serves 3–4

Chocolate with Two Flavours *right*

65 g/2½ oz bitter chocolate
200 ml/7 fl oz hot milk
2 teaspoons sugar
1 sachet lime tea
whipped cream
grated chocolate

Melt the chocolate very gradually in a little water over a low heat. Very gradually stir in the hot milk. Add the sugar and and stir until dissolved. Drop in the lime sachet and leave for 5 minutes to infuse. Remove the sachet and serve the chocolate very hot in a warmed heatproof glass. Top with whipped cream and sprinkle with grated chocolate.

Preparation time: 5 minutes, plus infusing
Cooking time: 5 minutes
Serves 1

Saffron Tea *top left*

1 teaspoon Chinese green tea
½ teaspoon saffron threads
900 ml/1½ pints water
sugar, to taste
4 lemon slices, to serve (optional)

Rinse a teapot with boiling water. Add the tea and saffron to the pot. Bring the water to the boil and immediately pour into the warmed pot. Leave to infuse for 5 minutes. Pour the tea through a strainer into warm glasses or cups. Add sugar to taste and decorate each glass or cup with a lemon slice, if liked.

Preparation time: 3 minutes, plus infusing
Cooking time: 5 minutes
Serves 4

Lemon Mint Tea

1 sachet mint tea
250 ml/8 fl oz boiling water
2 sugar lumps
1 lemon

Put the mint tea sachet in the boiling water and leave to infuse for 5 minutes. Rub the sugar lumps over a lemon until they absorb the oil from the zest. Remove the tea sachet from the infusion and add the sugar lumps. Serve hot in a handled glass.

Preparation time: 3 minutes, plus infusing
Serves 1

Jasmine Tea

Jasmine tea is highly perfumed. Serve with spicy dishes, or to refresh the palate after a meal.

1 tablespoon dried jasmine flowers
50 g/2 oz black Chinese leaf tea
boiling water

Mix the jasmine flowers with the leaf tea and store in an airtight container until required. To make the tea, place 1 teaspoon per person in a warmed pot and pour over boiling water. Leave for 2 minutes or longer, depending on the strength you prefer. Pour into small cups to serve.

Preparation time: 3 minutes, plus infusing
Serves 4

Camomile and Citrus Tea *bottom right*

1 sachet camomile tea
200 ml/7 fl oz boiling water
1 clove
juice of ½ orange
juice of ½ lemon
2 teaspoons honey
orange wedge, to serve

Put the camomile tea sachet in the boiling water and leave to infuse for 5 minutes. Discard the sachet and add the clove. Add the orange and lemon juices to a small pan with the honey. Heat gently and mix with the infusion. Remove the clove and serve in a warmed handled glass with an orange wedge.

Preparation time: 3 minutes, plus infusing
Serves 1

Smoothies and Juices

Drink to me only with thine eyes,
And I will pledge with mine;
Or leave a kiss but in the cup,
And I'll not look for wine.

Ben Jonson

(1573–1637)

Pink Melon Delight *top left*

65 g/2½ oz melon, cut into dice
65 g/2½ oz strawberries
1 scoop orange sorbet
150 ml/¼ pint ginger ale
strawberry, to decorate

Put the melon, strawberries and orange sorbet into a blender and blend at high speed for 15 seconds. Gently stir in the ginger ale, pour into a wine glass and decorate with a strawberry.

Preparation time: 4 minutes
Serves 2–3

Ginger and Vanilla Smoothie

3 scoops vanilla ice cream
50 ml/2 fl oz milk, chilled
100 ml/3½ fl oz orange juice
15 g/½ oz stem ginger in syrup
2 teaspoons ginger syrup
slices of stem ginger, to decorate

Put the ice cream and milk into a blender and add the orange juice, stem ginger and ginger syrup. Blend thoroughly and pour into 2 tall glasses. Decorate with a slice of stem ginger and serve with straws.

Preparation time: 4 minutes
Serves 2

Plum Shake

250 g/8 oz plums, skinned, stoned and roughly chopped
100 ml/3½ fl oz fresh orange juice
2 scoops vanilla ice cream

Place the plums and orange juice into a blender and add the ice cream. Blend thoroughly then pour into a large goblet. Serve with decorative straws.

Preparation time: 3 minutes
Serves 2

Banana Yogurt Shake

bottom right

600 ml/1 pint milk, chilled
2 large ripe bananas, peeled
300 ml/½ pint natural yogurt, chilled
2 tablespoons caster sugar
banana slices, to decorate

Put the milk, bananas, yogurt and caster sugar into a blender and process for 10–15 seconds until smooth. Pour into tall glasses, decorate with a slice of banana and serve immediately.

Preparation time: 3 minutes
Serves 2–4

Cranberry, Raspberry and Orange Crush *left*

200 ml/7 fl oz cranberry juice, chilled
100 ml/3½ fl oz fresh orange juice
250 ml/8 oz raspberries, chilled, plus extra for decorating
3 scoops orange sorbet, plus extra to serve (optional)
sugar, to taste (optional)

Put the cranberry juice, orange juice, raspberries and orange sorbet into a food processor or blender and process until frothy. Taste and add sugar if required. Serve in cocktail glasses with an extra scoop of sorbet if liked.

Preparation time: 4 minutes
Serves 2–3

Passion Fruit and Lime Cream

3 passion fruit, chilled
grated rind and juice of 2 limes
3 scoops vanilla ice cream
milk, to top up
sugar, to taste

Remove the pulp and seeds from the passion fruit, reserving some seeds for decoration. Put the fruit, lime rind, juice and ice cream into a food processor or blender and process until combined. Add milk and sugar to taste and serve decorated with the reserved passion fruit seeds.

Preparation time: 4 minutes
Serves 1–2

Papaya, Melon and Strawberry Smoothie

1 papaya, peeled, deseeded and quartered
250 g/8 oz honeydew melon, roughly chopped
6 large strawberries, hulled
150 ml/¼ pint coconut milk
sugar, to taste
crushed ice, to serve
strawberry slices, to decorate

Place the papaya and melon in a food processor or blender and blend until smooth. Add the strawberries, blend then add the coconut milk. Add sugar according to taste and serve in glasses over crushed ice, decorated with strawberry slices.

Preparation time: 5 minutes
Serves 2–3

Spiced Mango and Coconut Smoothie *right*

250 ml/8 fl oz canned coconut milk, chilled
150 ml/¼ pint semi-skimmed or skimmed milk, chilled
150 ml/¼ pint mango juice
1 large mango, peeled, stoned and roughly chopped
juice of 1 lime
1 teaspoon crushed cardamom seeds
sugar, to taste
crushed ice, to serve
mango slices, to decorate

Put the coconut milk, milk, mango juice, mango, lime juice and cardamom seeds into a food processor or blender and process until smooth. Taste and add sugar if required. Serve in tall glasses poured over crushed ice. Decorate with slices of mango.

Preparation time: 4 minutes
Serves 2

Cherry Thickshake *top left*

300 g/10 oz black cherries, pitted and halved, or tinned cherries
juice of 1 lemon
300 ml/½ pint vanilla ice cream
sugar, to taste
cherries, to decorate

Put the cherries in a food processor or blender with the lemon juice and ice cream and process until smooth. Taste and add sugar if required. Serve in tall glasses, decorated with whole cherries, if you wish.

Preparation time: 4 minutes
Serves 2–3

Banana Mocha Smoothie

100 ml/3½ fl oz espresso coffee, chilled
125 g/4 oz plain chocolate, melted
2 scoops vanilla ice cream
100 ml/3½ fl oz milk, chilled
2 ripe bananas
whipped cream, to serve
chocolate shavings, to decorate

Place the coffee and chocolate in a food processor or blender and blend until combined. Add the ice cream and milk and blend again. Add the bananas one at a time and blend until smooth. Cover and chill for 1 hour. Serve topped with whipped cream and decorated with chocolate shavings.

Preparation time: 10 minutes, plus chilling
Serves 2–3

Chocolate, Pear and Cinnamon Smoothie

2 ripe dessert pears, peeled, cored and quartered
3 scoops chocolate ice cream, extra for serving
1 teaspoon ground cinnamon
300 ml/½ pint milk, chilled

Put the pears into a food processor or blender and process for about 1 minute. Add the ice cream and the cinnamon and process again, then add the milk and process once more until smooth and creamy. Serve with a small scoop of chocolate ice cream floating on the top.

Preparation time: 5 minutes
Serves 3

Iced Strawberry and Banana Shake *bottom right*

250 g/8 oz strawberries, hulled and halved
1 small banana, sliced
1 scoop strawberry sorbet
2 scoops vanilla ice cream
100 ml/3½ fl oz milk, chilled
whipped cream, to serve (optional)
strawberry halves, to decorate

Put the strawberries, banana, sorbet, ice cream and milk into a food processor or blender and blend until smooth. Add more ice cream for a thicker shake, or more milk for a thinner drink, if you like. Serve in tall glasses topped with whipped cream and decorated with a strawberry half.

Preparation time: 5 minutes
Serves 2–3

Chocolate and Raspberry Shake *top left*

150 g/5 oz plain chocolate, broken into small pieces
250 g/8 oz raspberries
300 g/10 oz natural or Greek yogurt
sugar, to taste

TO SERVE:
crushed ice
chocolate curls (optional)
raspberries

Put the chocolate, raspberries and yogurt into a food processor or blender and process until smooth. Taste and add sugar if required. Serve in tall glasses over crushed ice and decorate with chocolate curls and raspberries, if you wish.

Preparation time: 5 minutes
Serves 2–3

Apple and Pecan Smoothie

50 g/2 oz shelled pecan nuts
250 g/8 oz natural yogurt
300 ml/½ pint apple juice
clear honey, to taste
ice cubes or crushed ice, to serve

Put the pecans into a food processor or blender with a few tablespoons of the yogurt and process to a paste. Add the remaining yogurt and the apple juice and process again until well mixed. Sweeten to taste with honey and serve with ice.

Preparation time: 5 minutes
Serves 2–3

Apricot, Raisin and Pistachio Smoothie

6 ready-to-eat dried apricots
50 g/2 oz raisins
25 g/1 oz pistachio nuts, shelled
250 ml/8 fl oz coconut milk
250 ml/8 fl oz apricot juice
sugar, to taste
ice cubes or crushed ice, to serve

Place the dried apricots, raisins and pistachios in a food processor or blender with a little of the coconut milk and process for 1 minute to make a smooth paste. Add the remaining coconut milk and the apricot juice and process until well mixed. Add sugar to taste and serve over ice.

Preparation time: 5 minutes
Serves 2

Peach Dream *bottom right*

250 g/8 oz peaches, skinned, stoned and roughly chopped
200 ml/7 fl oz Greek yogurt
100 ml/3½ fl oz skimmed milk
250 g/8 oz crushed ice
1 teaspoon clear honey, or to taste
toasted almonds, to decorate

Put the peaches, yogurt, milk, ice and honey into a food processor or blender and process until smooth. Taste, add more honey if required and process again. Pour into chilled glasses and decorate with toasted almonds.

Preparation time: 5 minutes
Serves 4

Kiwi, Grape and Lime Crush *left*

250 g/8 oz kiwi fruit
300 ml/½ pint white grape juice
juice of 2 limes
crushed ice, to serve
kiwi fruit slices, to decorate

Put the kiwi fruit, grape juice and lime juice into a food processor and blend until smooth. Serve in glasses over crushed ice and decorate with slices of kiwi fruit.

Preparation time: 5 minutes
Serves 3–4

Pineapple and Ginger Fizz

4 fresh pineapple slices
350 ml/12 fl oz traditional-style ginger beer
juice of 2 limes
crushed ice
mint sprigs, to decorate

Put the pineapple slices into a food processor or blender with 100 ml/3½ fl oz of the ginger beer and process until blended. Add the remaining ginger beer, the lime juice and the crushed ice and process again. Serve in tall glasses and decorate with mint sprigs.

Preparation time: 5 minutes
Serves 4

Cranberry, Apple and Grapefruit Cooler

250 ml/8 fl oz cranberry juice
250 ml/8 fl oz apple juice
100 ml/3½ fl oz fresh pink grapefruit juice
sparkling mineral water

Pour the cranberry, apple and grapefruit juices into a jug and mix together thoroughly. Chill in the refrigerator for at least 1 hour then top up with sparkling mineral water, stir and serve.

Preparation time: 5 minutes, plus chilling
Serves 2–3

Watermelon and Citrus Crush *right*

1 large or 2 small ripe watermelons, chilled
300 ml/½ pint fresh orange juice
juice of 1 lime
sugar, to taste
crushed ice, to serve
triangles of watermelon, to decorate

Cut the watermelon into quarters and remove the skin and seeds. Roughly chop the flesh and put it into a food processor with the orange juice and lime juice and process until smooth. Serve in glasses packed with crushed ice. Add a watermelon triangle to each glass to decorate.

Preparation time: 5 minutes
Serves 2–3

Peach, Pear and Raspberry Crush *top left*

1 ripe peach, skinned, stoned and roughly chopped
1 ripe dessert pear, peeled, cored and and roughly chopped
125 g/4 oz raspberries
200 ml/7 fl oz peach juice
250 ml/8 fl oz crushed ice
pear slices, to decorate (optional)

Put the peach, pear, raspberries and peach juice into a food processor or blender with the crushed ice and blend until smooth. Serve in cocktail glasses decorated with a pear slice, if you like.

Preparation time: 3 minutes
Serves 2–3

Carrot, Canteloupe and Citrus Cooler

250 g/8 oz canteloupe melon, quartered
250 ml/8 fl oz carrot juice, chilled
150 ml/¼ pint fresh orange juice
juice of 2 limes
crushed ice, to serve

Put the melon into a food processor or blender and process for 1 minute, then add the carrot, orange and lime juices and process again until thoroughly mixed. To serve pour into tall glasses over crushed ice.

Preparation time: 5 minutes
Serves 2–3

Orange and Papaya Fizz

1 papaya, peeled, quartered and deseeded
250 ml/8 fl oz fresh orange juice
4–6 ice cubes
sparkling mineral water
mint sprigs, to decorate

Place the papaya and orange juice in a food processor or blender and process for about 30 seconds until smooth. Put 2–3 ice cubes into 2 tall glasses, pour in the drink and top up with sparkling water. Stir and decorate with a mint sprig.

Preparation time: 5 minutes
Serves 2

Strawberry and Citrus Crush *bottom right*

50 g/2 oz strawberries, hulled and halved
100 ml/3½ fl oz pink grapefruit juice
100 ml/3½ fl oz orange juice
juice of 1 lemon
crushed ice, to serve

TO DECORATE:
strawberries, halved
lemon spirals

Put the strawberries into a food processor or blender with the grapefruit, orange and lemon juices and blend until smooth. To serve, fill glasses with crushed ice, pour in the drink and decorate with strawberries and lemon spirals.

Preparation time: 5 minutes
Serves 2

Coolers and Quenchers

If all the world were paper,
And all the sea were ink;
If all the trees were
bread and cheese
How should we do for drink?

Anonymous

(17th century)

Apple and Mint Lemonade *top left*

12–14 ice cubes
1 litre/1¾ pints apple juice
4 tablespoons fresh lemon juice
2 tablespoons chopped mint
still or sparkling mineral water

TO DECORATE:
mint sprigs
apple slices

Put the ice cubes into a jug and pour in the apple juice. Add the lemon juice and mint and stir to mix thoroughly. To serve, top up the jug with still or sparkling mineral water and decorate with mint sprigs and apple slices.

Preparation time: 4 minutes
Serves 6

Lemon Barley Water

rind of 1 lemon, cut into fine strips
2 tablespoons barley
1.2 litres/2 pints boiling water
sugar, to taste
ice cubes, to serve

TO DECORATE:
lemon rind
mint sprigs

Put the lemon rind into a heatproof jug with the barley. Pour over the boiling water and stir well. Cover and leave to stand overnight. Add sugar to taste, then strain the barley water through a piece of muslin – the barley water should be clear and pale yellow in colour. To serve, fill tall glasses with ice cubes, pour over the lemon barley water and decorate with fine strips of lemon rind and mint sprigs.

Preparation time: 10 minutes, plus standing
Serves 4

Elderflower Champagne

8 elderflower heads in full bloom, without leaves
juice of 2 lemons
750 g/1½ lb sugar
2 tablespoons white wine vinegar
5 litres/8 pints cold water

TO SERVE:
lemon slices
cucumber slices

Wash the elderflower blooms and put them into a large wide-necked jar. Squeeze the juice from the lemons into the jar then cut each lemon into quarters and add them too. Add the sugar and wine vinegar and pour over the cold water. Stir well, then cover and leave for 24 hours, stirring occasionally.

Strain the liquid into screw-top bottles, then leave them in a cool, dark place for 2 weeks.

Serve chilled, decorated with lemon and cucumber slices.

Preparation time: 20 minutes, plus standing and maturing
Makes 5 litres/8 pints

Lemonade *bottom right*

6 lemons
600 ml/1 pint water
125 g/4 oz sugar

TO SERVE:
crushed ice
chilled still or sparkling mineral water
lemon slices
mint sprigs

Grate the rind from the lemons – be careful to take just the zest and none of the white pith. Squeeze the lemon juice into a jug and reserve. Pour the water and sugar into a large saucepan and add the lemon rind. Stir until the sugar has dissolved, then boil for 5 minutes. Leave to cool, then stir in the lemon juice.

To serve, strain a little lemonade into glasses or into a jug. Add crushed ice and top up with chilled mineral water. Decorate with the lemon slices and mint.

Preparation time: 20 minutes, plus cooling
Serves 6

Saffron Lassi *top left*

This is a most refreshing drink for a hot summer day.

3 tablespoons milk
15 saffron threads, extra to decorate
½ teaspoon cumin seeds
300 ml/½ pint thick natural yogurt
¼ teaspoon salt
¼ teaspoon caster sugar
300 ml/½ pint water, chilled
cracked ice cubes, to serve

Pour the milk over the saffron threads and set aside for 1–2 hours to infuse. Heat a frying pan until hot then add the cumin seeds and toast for 1–2 minutes or until you can smell the cumin. Remove from the heat and leave to cool. Put the yogurt, salt, sugar and water into a food processor and blend for 30 seconds. Add the toasted cumin and blend for 1 minute. Add the soaked saffron and liquid to the yogurt mixture and blend briefly until combined. Fill a jug with cracked ice cubes, pour the lassi over the ice and serve decorated with saffron threads.

Preparation time: 10 minutes, plus infusing and cooling
Cooking time: about 3 minutes
Serves 4

Tutti Frutti Verbena Cocktail

3 sachets verbena tea
600 ml/1 pint boiling water
juice of 2 oranges
juice of 2 lemons
150 ml/¼ pint apricot juice
150 ml/¼ pint pineapple juice
a few ice cubes

Put the sachets of verbena tea into a heatproof jug, pour over the boiling water and leave to infuse. When the tea is cold, remove the sachets from the jug. Strain the tea into another jug and add the juice from the oranges and lemons, the apricot juice, pineapple juice and a few ice cubes.

Preparation time: 5 minutes, plus infusing
Serves 4–6

Iced Fruit Tea

600 ml/1 pint freshly brewed strong Indian tea
175 g/6 oz caster sugar
juice of 1 lemon
300 ml/½ pint fresh orange juice
10–12 ice cubes
75 g/3 oz strawberries, hulled and sliced
½ lemon, sliced
½ orange, sliced
mint sprigs, to decorate

Stir the tea and sugar in a jug until the sugar has dissolved. Add the lemon and orange juices then cover and chill for 1 hour. Pour the tea mixture into a punch bowl and add the ice cubes and sliced fruit. Decorate with mint sprigs to serve.

Preparation time: 5 minutes, plus chilling
Serves 4

Iced Coffee *bottom right*

600 ml/1 pint hot strong coffee
2 cinnamon sticks
1 teaspoon grated nutmeg
1 teaspoon ground ginger
rind of 1 lemon, cut into thin strips
rind of 1 orange, cut into thin strips
sugar, to taste
ice cubes
whipped cream, to serve
chocolate coffee beans, to decorate

Put the hot coffee into a heatproof jug with the cinnamon, nutmeg, ginger and lemon and orange rind. Stir well, then add sugar to taste. Cover and chill in the refrigerator for at least 1 hour. To serve, fill tall glasses with ice cubes or crushed ice, pour in the coffee and top with whipped cream and chocolate coffee beans, if you wish.

Preparation time: 10 minutes, plus chilling
Serves 6

Pineapple Cobbler *top left*

4–5 ice cubes
200 ml/7 fl oz pineapple juice
1 dash fresh lime juice
5 dashes Angostura bitters
bitter lemon
slice of fresh pineapple, to decorate

Put the ice cubes into a cocktail shaker and pour in the pineapple juice, lime juice and Angostura bitters. Shake then strain into a large wine glass and top up with bitter lemon. Decorate with a pineapple slice.

Preparation time: 4 minutes
Serves 1

Red Sombrero

4–5 ice cubes
1 measure fresh lemon juice
1 measure strawberry juice
1 measure fresh orange juice
1 measure pineapple juice
a few dashes grenadine
orange slice, to decorate

Put some ice cubes into a cocktail shaker and pour in the lemon juice, strawberry juice, orange juice and pineapple juice and add a few dashes of grenadine. Shake well and strain into a balloon glass. Decorate with an orange slice and serve with straws.

Preparation time: 5 minutes
Serves 1

Rhubarb Cooler

500 g/1 lb rhubarb, trimmed and cut into bite-sized chunks
300 ml/½ pint fresh orange juice
125 g/4 oz sugar
sparkling mineral water, chilled
ice cubes or crushed ice, to serve

Place the rhubarb and orange juice in a pan and bring to the boil. Lower the heat and simmer for a few minutes until the rhubarb is tender. Remove from the heat and leave to cool then add sugar to taste. Purée in a food processor or blender until smooth then chill in the refrigerator for at least 1 hour.

Serve in glasses, topped up with sparkling mineral water. Stir well to mix and add some ice cubes or crushed ice.

Preparation time: 8 minutes, plus cooling and chilling
Cooking time: 5 minutes
Serves 3–4

Grapefruit and Orange Cooler *bottom right*

1 sugar lump
1 orange
2 measures orange juice
2 measures grapefruit juice
crushed ice or ice cubes

Rub the sugar lump over the orange rind until it absorbs the oil from the zest. Put the sugar lump in a tumbler. Stir the orange and grapefruit juices with the ice. Strain into the tumbler and top up with soda water. Add more crushed ice and serve with straws.

Preparation time: 5 minutes
Serves 1

Guavarama *left*

crushed ice
200 ml/7 fl oz guava juice
2 teaspoons fresh lime juice
4 teaspoons blackcurrant syrup
5 dashes rum essence
melon slice, to decorate

Put some crushed ice into a blender and add the guava juice, lime juice, blackcurrant syrup and rum essence. Blend thoroughly then strain into a chilled cocktail glass and decorate with a melon slice.

Preparation time: 4 minutes
Serves 1

Honeymoon

crushed ice
1 measure maple syrup or clear honey
4 teaspoons fresh lime juice
1 measure fresh orange juice
1 measure apple juice

TO DECORATE:
twist of orange rind
cocktail cherry

Put some crushed ice into a cocktail shaker and add the maple syrup or honey, lime juice, orange juice and apple juice. Shake well then strain into a chilled cocktail glass. Decorate with an orange twist and a cherry on a cocktail stick.

Preparation time: 4 minutes
Serves 1

Catherine Blossom

200 ml/7 fl oz fresh orange juice
2 teaspoons maple syrup
2 scoops orange sorbet
soda water

Put the orange juice, maple syrup and orange sorbet into a blender and blend for 15 seconds. Pour into a tall glass and top up with soda water.

Preparation time: 4 minutes
Serves 1

Tomato and Cucumber Cooler *right*

crushed ice
150 ml/¼ pint tomato juice
25 g/1 oz cucumber, peeled
2 dashes lemon juice
2 dashes Worcestershire sauce
salt and pepper
slice of cucumber, to decorate

Put a little crushed ice into a blender. Add the tomato juice, cucumber, lemon juice, Worcestershire sauce and salt and pepper to taste and blend well. Frost a cocktail glass with salt. Pour in the drink and decorate with a slice of cucumber on the rim.

Preparation time: 3 minutes
Serves 1

Party Punches

If all be true that I do think,
There are five reasons
we should drink;
Good wine – a friend –
or being dry –
Or lest we should be by
and by – Or any other
reason why.

Henry Aldrich
(1647–1710)

Bellini *top left*

3–4 ripe peaches, skinned, stoned and chilled
2–3 teaspoons sugar
1 bottle Champagne, chilled

Put the peaches into a food processor and blend to a purée then turn the purée into a large bowl and add the sugar. Pour in the chilled Champagne and stir well, then strain into 6 chilled cocktail glasses.

Preparation time: 5 minutes
Serves 6

White Wine Punch

ice
300 ml/ ½ pint extra dry sherry
4 tablespoons pernod
4 tablespoons brandy
2 bottles dry white wine
rind of 1 lemon
soda water

Put several large chunks of ice into a punch bowl. Pour the sherry, pernod, brandy and wine over the ice, add the lemon rind and stir thoroughly. Cover the bowl and chill in the refrigerator for at least 1 hour. Top up with soda water just before serving.

Preparation time: 10 minutes, plus chilling
Serves 12–14

West Indian Punch

juice of 4 grapefruit or 600 ml/1 pint canned unsweetened grapefruit juice
juice of 2 oranges
2 tablespoons sugar syrup
2 teaspoons Angostura bitters
ice
½ bottle brandy
4 tablespoons Bénédictine
1 bottle dark rum
grated nutmeg
rind of 1 lemon, to decorate

Put the grapefruit juice, orange juice, sugar syrup and bitters into a punch bowl and stir thoroughly then add several large chunks of ice. Pour the brandy, Bénédictine and rum over the ice. Stir thoroughly and sprinkle lavishly with nutmeg. Chill in the refrigerator for at least 1 hour. Decorate with lemon rind to serve.

Preparation time: 15 minutes, plus chilling
Serves 12–14

Chablis Cup *bottom right*

3 ripe peaches, skinned and sliced
1 orange, cut into thin slices
cocktail cherries
3 teaspoons sugar
1 bottle chablis
4 measures Grand Marnier
4 measures kirsch

Put the peaches, orange slices, cherries and sugar into a punch bowl. Pour in the chablis, Grand Marnier and kirsch and stir thoroughly. Cover the bowl and chill in the refrigerator for 1 hour. Serve in goblets.

Preparation time: 5–10 minutes, plus chilling
Serves 6

Golden Rum Punch *top left*

50 g/2 oz sugar
1 litre/1¾ pints pineapple juice
juice of 6 oranges
juice of 6 lemons
1 bottle golden rum
ice
1 litre/1¾ pints ginger ale or soda water

TO DECORATE:
fruit in season, such as pineapples, oranges, cherries and strawberries, sliced

Put the sugar into a punch bowl, pour in the pineapple juice and stir to dissolve the sugar. Add the orange and lemon juices and pour in the rum. Stir to mix. Put a large block of ice into the punch bowl and leave the punch to get really cold.

When you are ready to serve, pour in the ginger ale or soda water. Decorate with slices of pineapple and orange, cherries, strawberries and any other fruit in season.

Preparation time: 20–30 minutes, plus chilling
Serves 20

Burgundy Punch

ice
1 bottle red burgundy
100 ml/3½ fl oz ruby port
60 ml/2½ fl oz fresh orange juice
2 teaspoons lemon juice
1 litre/1¾ pints iced water
3 tablespoons sugar

TO DECORATE:
orange slices
cocktail cherries

Put a large piece of ice into a punch bowl and pour in the burgundy, port, orange juice, lemon juice and iced water. Add the sugar and stir well. Decorate with orange slices and cherries and serve in large goblets.

Preparation time: 10–15 minutes
Serves 10

Sangria

1 bottle red wine
2 measures brandy
2 measures Cointreau
juice of 1 orange
juice of ½ lemon
4 teaspoons sugar
1 spiral of orange rind
1 spiral of lemon rind
10 ice cubes
300 ml/½ pint soda water

TO DECORATE:
orange and lemon slices
peach and apricot slices, if in season

Pour the red wine, brandy, Cointreau, orange juice and lemon juice into a 2 litre/3½ pint jug and add the sugar and orange and lemon rind. Chill in the refrigerator for at least 1 hour.

To serve, add the ice cubes and top up with soda water to taste. Decorate with orange and lemon slices and peaches and apricots, if available. Stir well and serve in wine glasses.

Preparation time: 10 minutes, plus chilling
Serves 6

Cider Cup *bottom right*

1 measure maraschino
1 measure orange Curaçao
1 measure brandy
1.2 litres/2 pints medium or dry cider
10–12 ice cubes
apple slices, to serve

Pour the maraschino, orange Curaçao, brandy and cider into a large glass jug or bowl. Add the ice and stir gently. Serve with apple slices.

Preparation time: 10 minutes
Serves 6

Orange and Peach Fizz *left*

2 litres/3½ pints sparkling white grape juice
1 litre/1¾ pints fresh orange juice
1 litre/1¾ pints peach juice
20–30 ice cubes
orange slices, to decorate

Pour the grape juice, orange juice and peach juice into a large punch bowl and stir well to mix. Carefully add the ice cubes, then decorate with orange slices.

Preparation time: 5 minutes
Serves about 20

Ginger Beer Punch

2 litres/3½ pints ginger beer
500 ml/17 fl oz apple juice
1 litre/1¾ pints homemade lemonade (**see page 78****)**
20–30 ice cubes

TO DECORATE:
cucumber slices
halved strawberries
mint sprigs

Pour the ginger beer, apple juice and lemonade into a punch bowl and stir to mix. Add the ice, then float the cucumber slices and strawberries on top and add the mint sprigs.

Preparation time: 10 minutes
Serves 20

Non-Alcoholic Sangria

1 litre/1¾ pints orange juice
50 g/2 oz sugar
2 litres/3½ pints red grape juice
juice of 6 lemons
juice of 6 limes
20–30 ice cubes
orange, lemon and lime slices, to decorate

Pour the orange juice and sugar into a punch bowl and stir until the sugar dissolves. Add the grape juice, lemon juice and lime juice and stir thoroughly to mix. Add the ice, then float the fruit slices on top.

Preparation time: 10 minutes
Serves 20

Apple and Strawberry Cup *right*

500 g/1 lb very ripe strawberries, hulled
2 tablespoons caster sugar
juice of 1 large orange
sparkling apple juice
ice cubes

Place the strawberries in a bowl and bruise them with a wooden spoon. Sprinkle with the sugar and orange juice, then cover and leave to stand for 1 hour. Pour the fruit cup into a jug, top it up with sparkling apple juice and ice cubes and serve.

Preparation time: 10 minutes, plus standing
Serves 6

Spiced Ginger Punch

top left

2 oranges
cloves, to taste
1 cm/½ inch piece of fresh root ginger, peeled and grated
2 litres/3½ pints ginger ale
10 cm/4 inch cinnamon stick

Stud the oranges with the cloves, then bake them in a preheated oven at 180°C/350°F/Gas Mark 4 for about 25 minutes, until they are a rich golden colour. Cut the oranges into slices with a sharp knife then put them into a saucepan with the grated ginger, ginger ale and cinnamon stick. Bring steadily to boiling point, but do not boil. Remove the cinnamon stick then pour the punch into heat-proof glasses or mugs.

Preparation time: 10 minutes
Cooking time: about 30 minutes
Serves 12

Heartwarmer

200 ml/7 fl oz red grape juice
250 g/8 oz brown sugar
350 ml/12 fl oz dark rum
1.5 litres/2½ pints dry white wine
450 ml/¾ pint red wine

Put the grape juice into a saucepan, add the sugar and stir over a gentle heat until the sugar has dissolved completely. Stir in the dark rum and set aside. Pour the white wine and red wine into a large saucepan and heat until hot but not boiling. Add the rum and grape juice mixture and stir together. Serve hot.

Preparation time: 5 minutes
Cooking time: 10 minutes
Serves 12

Mulled Wine

150 ml/¼ pint water
8 cloves
2 x 10 cm/4 inch cinnamon sticks
1 tablespoon brown sugar
1 lemon, thinly sliced
1 bottle red wine
150 ml/¼ pint port (optional)

Put the water, cloves, cinnamon sticks and sugar into a large saucepan and boil for 5 minutes. Add the lemon slices then remove the pan from the heat and leave to infuse for 10 minutes. Add the wine and heat slowly for 5 minutes, to just below simmering point. Add the port, if using, and serve hot, in warmed heatproof glasses or mugs.

Preparation time: 5 minutes, plus infusing
Cooking time: 10 minutes
Serves 6

Christmas Cup *bottom right*

1 bottle light red wine
10 cm/4 inch cinnamon stick
3–5 cloves
125 g/4 oz sugar
rind of ¼ lemon, chopped
50 g/2 oz blanched almonds
50 g/2 oz seedless raisins

Pour the wine into a saucepan, add the cinnamon and cloves and simmer for about 5 minutes over a low heat. Add sugar, lemon rind, almonds and raisins, stir and simmer for another 5 minutes. Serve in warmed heatproof glasses.

Preparation time: 5 minutes
Cooking time: 10 minutes
Serves 4–6

Special Photography:
Bill Reavell
Jacket Photography:
Bill Reavell
Cocktail Preparation/Styling:
Lucie Southgate
at The North Pole
131 Greenwich High Road
Greenwich